WHEN A THUG MEETS JESUS

WHEN A THUG MEETS JESUS

MACK HUGHLEY

J MERRILL

J Merrill Publishing, Inc.
434 Hillpine Drive
Columbus, OH 43207
www.JMerrill.pub

ISBN-13: 978-1-961475-97-7 (Paperback)
ISBN-13: 978-1-961475-98-4 (eBook)

Book Title: When A Thug Meets Jesus
Author: Mack Hughley

CONTENTS

1

Hello, my name is Mack Hughley. I want to start by saying I once was a thug, not knowing I would meet Jesus. When you live like a thug, you might lose your life or end up in jail. You don't think about it that way when living on the streets. All you can see are the things you go through being a thug. Often, a thug is a person who doesn't really know who he is, so he puts up an image in front of a friend or a crowd of people just to maintain his thug status. Deep down inside, he is hurting and doesn't know how to change. He is looking for a way to come out of being a thug.

Sometimes, you can get lonely trying to be someone you are not. So, you wrestle with the thug image because you don't want the people you are associated with to think you are soft. When you call yourself a thug, people don't understand. People don't know the mind of a thug. Some thugs are depressed and want to take their own lives. Sometimes, they become this person who has gotten so drawn away that he doesn't know who he is anymore. The thug lives a fake life, trying to impress people who don't care if he gets ahead in life or not. The thug always tries to show the world that he can still bully and push people around. That said, a thug always thinks he has to prove himself to fit in. He may make a statement in front of people, saying, "I'm going to shoot all of them that were laughing at me," without asking, "What are you laughing at?" He just takes matters into his own hands without considering that many people may lose their lives over a thug fabricating a situation in his mind.

But when the thug meets Jesus, he must learn to humble himself, something he never knew how to do. This experience that he comes up against with Jesus is new for him because he has always been in control. Jesus has authority over the situation, so the thug tries to wrestle with something he can't see. The thug can feel the presence of someone with more authority than he has, but still can't see him. This is when the power of God takes over the thug. He is in a place where he can't hurt anyone, kill anymore, or threaten anyone. It's like being in handcuffs. Understanding that when the law puts handcuffs on him, he sees and feels those, but spiritually, when Jesus puts handcuffs on a thug, he also can feel them but can't see them. He's up against something he can't see and no longer has the upper hand. This is the turning point in a thug's life.

2

The thug doesn't understand everything that is happening wrong in his life that he is trying to fight. He is trying to fight against the turning point. The thug doesn't know that Jesus is trying to step into his life because there is no guidance. Great trials keep coming up against the thug. Things keep worsening in his life to where he is ready to give up. When you don't know how to handle things when you have been a thug from the street, you turn to things in the street that you did not try before, such as drugs. You never used them before, so now you understand you hit rock bottom. You're at your breaking point. This is when a thug meets Jesus. He has to be broken first to understand who he is dealing with; he must have a one-on-one experience with Jesus. I will give you an example of what I'm talking about from a biblical point of view.

Let's look at this man named Saul (who is considered to be a thug) in the Bible. Pay attention to this passage, Acts 9:1–6 (KJV):

"And Saul, yet breathing out threatenings and slaughter against the disciples of the Lord, went unto the high priest, And desired of him letters to Damascus to the synagogues, that if he found any of this way, whether they were men or women, he might bring them bound unto Jerusalem. And as he journeyed, he came near Damascus: and suddenly there shined round about him a light from heaven: And he fell to the earth, and heard a voice saying unto him, Saul, Saul, why persecutest thou me? And he said, Who art thou, Lord? And the Lord said, I am Jesus whom thou persecutest: it is hard for thee to kick against the pricks. And he trembling and astonished said, Lord, what wilt thou have me to do? And the Lord said unto him, Arise, and go into the city, and it shall be told thee what thou must do."

This thug (Saul) had lost his eyesight because of the persecution he had inflicted on the church. Saul was struck down and blinded. His friends led him to a spiritual man's house named Ananias. Ananias told Saul that God wanted him to lay his hands on Saul. After Ananias had laid his hands on this young man, Saul received his sight. Not only did Saul receive his sight, but he also became one of the greatest ministers in the gospel. He became Paul, one of the greatest apostles spoken of in Bible history. This proves there is hope for a thug. While going through your transition, remember, that God can do all things (see Luke 1:37, KJV).

What this thug in the Bible experienced was the power of God that he was trying to fight against. Saul felt that if he found anyone praying in Jesus' name, he could bring them back bound, but it didn't work like that. There comes a time when you must decide whether you will accept death or Jesus. As we see the thug cry out, asking what he must do, he understands he has no control, and neither does he have power over the situation. As you can see, I used this great man in the Bible who was a thug until he met Jesus. His name was Saul, but God changed his name to Paul, just as he changed my name from "Peanut" to Pastor Hughley.

My brothers and sisters, it's not so much about me but what Jesus is saying to you now. This brother's life story he is living before you is all he never lived in Jesus. And what Jesus is saying to you is don't let this example pass you by without acknowledging what has happened right before you. Don't let arrogance stop you from accepting the absolute truth that is going on in this man's life. A man who sat with you, drank and smoked with you, cursed and ran with you, was with different women. This is the one God struck down to show himself as an example, to lead people with a thug mentality out of the snares of bondage. I believe God has a plan for man, and that is His great salvation. God gives us the ability to choose what's right from wrong. I believe and know that when we make that choice, shackles and chains will be broken. Young men will be set free from the hands of the enemy.

We need more men to come out and help our younger brothers who are suffering with who they are because of low self-esteem. We need to take away the power of the thug, trying to control them and rob them of the life that God has designed for man. God has always had a plan for us. It takes someone who has been down that road as a thug to relate to those who think there is no hope for them. With God, there is always hope. Trust those in that place where they once had the mind of a thug to take the time to show you how God worked it out for them.

We need more brothers to share their experiences with God so that our brothers battling in their minds and are ready to do something wrong will know there is a way out when God has delivered us from the same mind as a thug. Your cravings want to hurt and take away life from innocent people because you don't understand who you are. It wasn't until I met Jesus that I realized I was a man looking for direction. That's when I found out who I was.

Without good direction, my sisters and brothers, we can't be led out of captivity. It will take a thug to meet Jesus to be set free. It's going to take a thug to deliver a thug. Let us take on the newness of life to teach other men that we don't have to live with a thug mentality. It's time for real men to cry out and come out of what society says we can't come out of. I believe God will send help when He sees your hurt and is making you ready to change for the good. It took jail and soul searching to lead me to the house of God.

When we are going through this, we don't believe our breakthrough is in the house of God. Your mind will think about it. But when the right person is sent your way and takes time to pour into you, you feel the assurance in them. Because that person has been a thug, even though it's hard to trust, the Lord sends His great assurance through somebody just like you. All the thug mentality goes out the window.

3

So, long story short, and to bring this to a close, God has preserved me the same way He preserved the great Apostle Paul. I once was blinded and led the wrong way. But God still had grace and mercy over my life until He touched me. My eyes opened, and I realized I needed something greater. The Bible says, "Ye are of God, little children, and have overcome them: because greater is He that is in you, than he that is in the world" (1 John 4:4, KJV). So, when my eyes opened, my life opened as a man of God—no longer a thug.

I can remember growing up in the hood. I was in the fifth grade. I was drinking alcohol, and I believe alcohol played a part in my learning disability. I thought I was not normal like the other children and was angry. I didn't want to be in school or be around the other kids because of the classroom I had to be in all day. I started to be rebellious and do things that were not appropriate for a twelve-year-old child.

My mother raised me coming up, and my father wasn't in the home. So, I did everything in the street of that nature and started learning how to do inappropriate things at sixteen. I sold drugs, started stealing, and became rebellious at home. I was just disobedient and became angry because of the things I had to endure by not having my father in the home with me. I was misled by older people and picked up bad habits that led me to a place that almost cost me my life. Guns had been put to my head. I have been robbed as a thug.

You will face some of the same things you do to people. It will come back to you. I dropped out of school in the twelfth grade to fit in the street. I started staying out all night, selling drugs every day to the point my mother told me if I didn't change, I could be put out of the home. I had a sister and a brother, and I wasn't showing them how to be a good role model. I have three other brothers and two other sisters; I was never in their life. I never got to see them much, and when I saw them, I tried to buy them.

I wasn't trying to spend time with them because my mind was set on the things on the street. All I could see was how to take from people. I didn't have time for them growing up as a thug. It messed with me mentally. Sometimes, I thought I was going to die. I was strange when I was out there. I would see things that would happen before they happened. I would tell people things that would happen to them, and they happened. I wasn't taking that part seriously because I was focused on getting the next dollar, the next high, talking to the next female, or what party I was going to. This is the thug mentality that I lived for.

One day, I was standing outside, and the police rolled up. I had a pocket full of drugs, and things started going downhill for me. I caught a drug case. I had to go back and forth to court, not knowing or understanding what was happening. This was the first time I had been in the system for anything. So now the life of a thug has caught up with me, the turning point of my life. So now, I was sentenced to a year and a half in prison. There, I learned how to become a man and where my life goes when I leave. So, within that year and a half, I read the word of God while I was there. I remember my aunt giving me a scripture to read daily; I believe it was Psalm 23. I read that scripture every day before I went to bed and early in the morning, unaware she was sowing seeds.

So, when I got out, I got a job and worked for about six months. I started hanging around some of the same people and caught another case. I ran from the case for almost five years. I got another job; I was hiding by working. I knew that the law wasn't looking for a thug to work a job. The job kept me out of the streets. I would go out only on Saturdays.

One Saturday, I met this woman who changed my life. She had such a great heart, and she said some things to me that made me change my life. I started going to church with this woman, who I can now say is my beautiful wife, Debra Hughley. We dated for about three years and got married. I was still on the run from the law.

I gave my life to Christ in 2002. The only thing in my life was that I still had this black spot. I didn't want my three beautiful children to know their father was a thug and did terrible things growing up. One day, I remember my children saying, "Dad, stay in with us." I said, "I am just going to the store." I left the house with the wrong tags on the car, and the police pulled me over. When they ran my name, they said, "We have been looking for you."

So now I am back in the courthouse. Remember, I gave my life to Christ; the only thing left was the old case I was running from. But this time, it was different. A thug had met Jesus, and with that being said, my attitude was different. My character was different.

I was looking at six years. The Judge said, "Where have you been?" I said, "Judge, I have been working. I have been in church. My life has completely turned around since the time I was incarcerated. I'm married. I have children. I have my home. I even have a business and still have a job. I am a deacon in the church now."

The Judge asked, "Where is your church?" I said, "On 131st and Cane." She said, "I know that church." When she said that, I said, "Thank you, Lord. You are the God that sits on the throne."

My life has been changed ever since. I'm no longer a thug but a man of God standing on God's promises. I wouldn't change it for anything. God has done the impossible for me and my family. I got time served in community service. The difference was when I returned, I knew Jesus and favor were on my side. And God has rewarded me to become a pastor of a beautiful church in Cleveland, Ohio. There is hope for thugs as well.

So, a thug is one who commits criminal acts and does violent things to people. I remember growing up and doing things that would bring trouble to the home because I had violated someone's space. I had taken something from someone's house. And this was a part of me acting out because I didn't have my dad in the house. My mom was the one I had to look up to.

I may not have done some things that I have learned. I can remember sitting in a place with older people who were drinking. I was wondering what that tasted like. I was curious, so I asked for a drink. They told me no, but I kept asking and asking. Finally, someone gave me a drink, and I liked how it tasted and began to drink. I wanted more of what they had, so I no longer wanted to be around those who introduced me to stealing. I wanted to be around the older crowd, doing something different from those who introduced me to stealing and taking. So now, I have moved on to another stage in my life, still having problems as a young man. So now the drinking has taken me to the streets. I started out stealing, and now my drinking leads me to want to sell drugs because my friends were selling drugs. Now, I want to know what it's like to sell drugs. So now I take on the role of a drug dealer, and sometimes, I will get robbed while standing in places where I shouldn't be.

My mother does not know where I am because I was never home. My mother worried about her child and didn't know if I was alive. She hasn't heard from me, and when I showed up, I'd be disrespectful and unruly to her. She's still hurting and worrying about her child and doesn't know if I'm making it or what my health issues are. Then I showed up disrespectfully, conducted things I thought were popular, had a smart mouth with my parents, and took me to places I couldn't get out of myself. I was leaning towards a falling pit and didn't have a mind to want to change.

I would take the same issues inside the classroom because of how I was living, and I thought that if I went into this classroom with this approach, I could get the best grades. It didn't work, and I dropped out of school in the twelfth grade. I wanted to fit in the streets, so I started living the life of a thug. I would try to be popular and wanted to be accepted by a person or a group. That acceptance took me to places that I never thought I would be. I went to jail and prison and spent most of my life trying to return to where I should have been at an early age. It messed me up mentally and spiritually. I was in a bad state and would not be here to talk about it if I had not chosen to change.

I remember having a cousin tutor me at the table with my homework, and I can say things got better when I went to class. I understood what the teachers were saying. I knew how to read, count, and everything else. The only thing that troubled me was that I didn't know how to spell words well. That's what bothered me. Sometimes, this would trouble me and keep me from going to class. This would be a challenge for me. These are the things that I would have to fight against. But once I understood everyone starts from somewhere, I started pursuing the things of life that would reroute me from where I couldn't learn certain things in school.

I remember joining a church where the pastor, his wife, the ministers, and the deacons sat down with me and taught me. I understood some things that school could not teach me. I'm not ashamed to say that I went through all these obstacles in my life to get to where I am. I've just learned how to become a man. When I got to a place where maturity was, I'm not afraid to say that I met Debra, my wife, who played a big part in my life change. I'm so grateful for my parents, Mack and Dorothy. I remember going to places looking for a change and to all the clubs, thinking that change would be there. I remember meeting many people, thinking they had the right answers to my problems. But I was steadily getting hurt. One day, I realized I had this church family. I met people who opened their arms to me, and I am now learning a way of life. I am learning how to conduct myself as a man, and how to walk the right life.

4

So, one of the greatest things that happened to me... As a child, I wanted this to happen when I became an adult. When I got together, my father, who wasn't in the home, visited me when I became a pastor, and he stopped drinking alcohol. He put it down. He became a deacon in the church. He became one of the greatest men in the house of God. He could get four years sober and clean and level-headed, not only that. The good part was he found out who Jesus Christ was before he left the earth. He had a relationship with God. He had a relationship with me. Things had been restored coming from a thug. I could have died in the streets like that, but God had a plan for such a time as this. I'm telling you it's worth going through this life as long as God keeps breathing breath in your body. Don't give up on your children. Keep praying for them, keep pushing them. I can even say that even while writing this book, someone pushed me; a great author and publisher pushed me to pursue this message. I'm pleased with that, and I'm so grateful, and I'm thankful for all my brothers and sisters. I'm so grateful for them all. I love them all, and I wouldn't change it for anything. I am so grateful for my children and grandchildren, and I thank God for the woman who always saw the best in me; her name is Geneva Hughley.

I spent most of my time at her house. My mom would be at work through the night. So, I would go to school from there. I had been exposed to alcohol down the street at my auntie's house. I remember my one auntie saying, "Mama, this boy is drunk." I would argue with my aunt and say she doesn't know what she's talking about, Grandma. Grandma would ask, "Are you drunk?" I would say no, and she would say, "Go to bed," knowing that my auntie was right. I still would say she didn't know what she was talking about.

I would do this every day until the weekend came. I was with my mother on the weekend. On the weekdays, I would get drunk. Grandmother did not know; Mother had no idea. I was hiding. Teachers told my mother, "He is not keeping up with the other children." It was because the alcohol was messing with my mindset. I couldn't comprehend like the others because I was hungover, not knowing I was hungover, thinking I was still sleepy. Mother still doesn't know to this day. As I got older, I saw how I robbed myself of where I could have been. But this is the life of one who had become a thug.

After trying all these things, I finally got tired. I was walking down the street one night. It was so boring outside. No one was walking on the street but me and this lady. I saw her on the other side of the street. I was walking down to the neighborhood bar. There was a man named Mr. Taylor in the bar. He was an ex-cop, and he said, "Peanut, aren't you married now?" I said yes. He said, "Why are you out here? There's nothing out here for you. You're going to get back in trouble. So go home."

I walked back out of the bar and back down the street. I ran into this lady again. I said, "Hey, next time I see you, I will be a changed man. I hope you'll be a changed woman." The next time I saw that lady, I was a man of God, and she had just gotten out of prison. She had changed her life, too. She had started all over after that. My life had changed for the good, and there was no looking back. I had done what the world said I couldn't— change for the good. Believe it or not, I have changed so many lives just by changing my life. It's beautiful when you can see someone else change their life by looking at someone else's past; that was a thug who finally got his life back that was robbed from him as a kid and a teenager's life. He now helps men, women, children, and young adults. It was all in God's timing.

ABOUT THE AUTHOR

Mack Hughley experienced a spiritual awakening and was filled with the Holy Ghost on January 13, 2002. Soon after, he joined Pentecostal Determine COG, solidifying his commitment to his faith. From 2003 to 2005, Mack served faithfully as a deacon within the church. Feeling a divine calling, he stepped into ministry as a minister in 2006, preaching his first sermon in December of that year.

His dedication didn't go unnoticed. In 2011, he was ordained an elder of Pentecostal Determine COG, assuming a vital leadership role. Throughout these years, he was not only a faithful armor-bearer and assistant to Bishop W.B. Hanna but also a committed student at the PDC Bible College Institute, where he was nurtured under the careful directorship and tutelage of Bishop W.B. Hanna.

In March 2015, Elder Mack Hughley answered God's call to become a pastor. He organized the Rose of Sharon Church of God with five devoted believers. His guidance and commitment have led to the continual growth of the church, with new members joining every day.

On a personal note, Mack Hughley married Debra Hughley on April 8, 2000. The blessed union has resulted in three beautiful children: Laquise, Dexter, and Angel. The family's faith has been a cornerstone in their lives, and God's grace continues to bless them.

Reflecting on his spiritual journey, Mack Hughley stands firmly on the promises of God. He lives by Psalm 37:23: "The steps of a good man are ordered by the LORD: and he delighteth in his way." His faith and leadership continue to inspire those around him as he moves forward, guided by divine wisdom. Mack Hughley was saved and filled with the Holy Ghost on January 13, 2002, and joined Pentecostal Determine COG in 2002. He became a faithful deacon from 2003 to 2005. God called Elder Hughley into ministry as a minister in 2006. He preached his first sermon in December 2006. In 2011, he was ordained an elder of Pentecostal Determine COG. He has been a faithful armor-bearer and assistant to Bishop W.B. Hanna. He also attended the PDC Bible College Institute under the directorship and tutelage of Bishop W.B. Hanna. God called Elder Mack Hughley to pastor, and he answered the call in March 2015. Pastor Hughley and five believers organized the Rose of Sharon Church of God. God is adding to the church daily.

Mack Hughley married Debra Hughley on April 8, 2000. They have three children: Laquise, Dexter, and Angel. God has blessed this union.

Psalm 37:23 says, *"The steps of a good man are ordered by the LORD: and he delighteth in his way."* So, he is standing on the promises of God.

Printed in the USA
CPSIA information can be obtained
at www.ICGtesting.com
LVHW021131221123
764524LV00071B/2776

9 781961 475977